DO YOU REALLY WANT TO VISIT VENUS?

BY THOMAS K. ADAMSON

ILLUSTRATED BY DANIELE FABBRI

amicus illustrated

Amicus Illustrated is published by Amicus
P.O. Box 1329, Mankato, MN 56002
www.amicuspublishing.us

Library of Congress Cataloging-in-Publication Data
Adamson, Thomas K., 1970–
Do you really want to visit Venus? / by Thomas K.
Adamson ; illustrated by Daniele Fabbri. — 1st ed.
p. cm. — (Do you really want to visit—?)
Summary: "A child astronaut takes an imaginary trip
to Venus, learns about the extremely hot and harsh
conditions on the planet, and decides that Earth is a good
home after all. Includes solar system diagram, Venus vs.
Earth fact chart, and glossary"—Provided by publisher.
 Includes bibliographical references.
ISBN 978-1-60753-196-8 (library binding) —
ISBN 978-1-60753-402-0 (ebook)
1. Venus (Planet)—Juvenile literature. 2. Venus (Planet)—
Exploration—Juvenile literature. I. Fabbri, Daniele, 1978–
ill. II. Title. III. Series: Do you really want to visit—?
 QB621.A328 2014
 523.42–dc23   2012025970

Editor: Rebecca Glaser
Designer: The Design Lab

Printed in the United States of America at
Corporate Graphics in North Mankato, Minnesota.

Date 4/2014 PO 1219

9 8 7 6 5 4 3

So you think you want to go to Venus? The planet has huge volcanoes. You'd win the science fair for sure. But do you *really* want to go to there?

Venus is the closest planet to Earth. But the last space probe still took five months to get there.

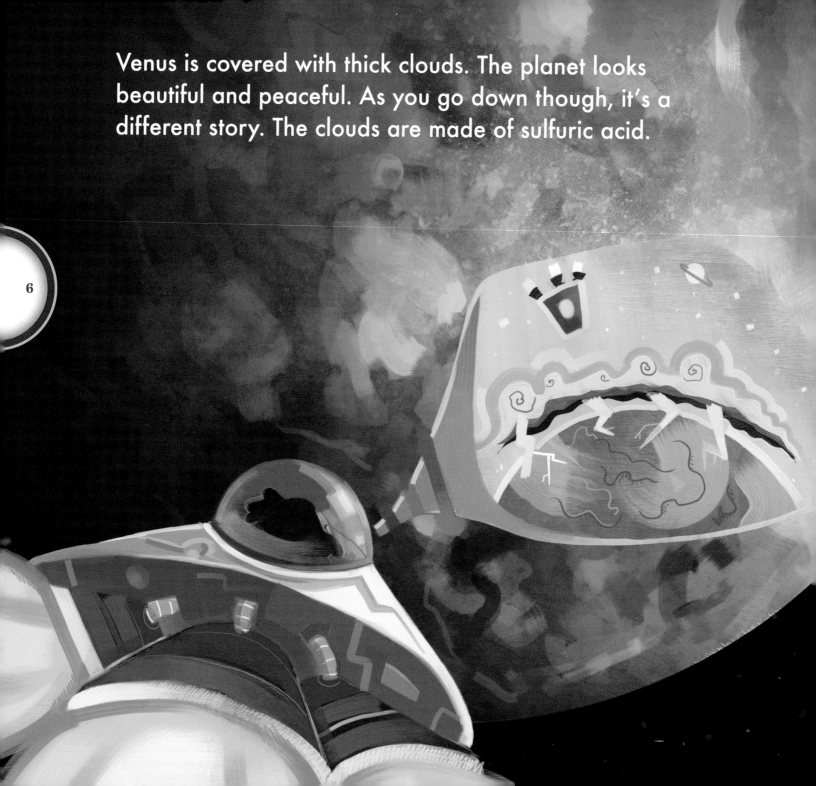

Venus is covered with thick clouds. The planet looks beautiful and peaceful. As you go down though, it's a different story. The clouds are made of sulfuric acid.

When you land, the air is almost twice as hot as an oven. You put on a super-thick, crush-proof space suit. Without it, the heavy air could squash you like a bug.

7

The Sun's light through the clouds appears red. It's like a sunset in the middle of the day. And because it's so cloudy, there are no shadows.

Most of the area is flat, but you look off into the distance. You see a hazy mountain looming over the plains and zoom over to get a closer look.

This volcano is huge. Maat Mons is four times wider than the biggest volcano on Earth.

11

After getting a lava sample, you keep exploring. Is that snow on a volcano?

It's frozen metal. Some volcanoes erupt fine pieces of metal, which settle as frost. Good thing you brought your snowboard.

13

Your space suit can't hold out in the heat much longer. Should you wait for night? Don't bother. It will still be hotter than an oven.

The clouds hold in the heat. They create a massive greenhouse effect. And the sun won't set for about 59 Earth days. Time to get off this blistering surface.

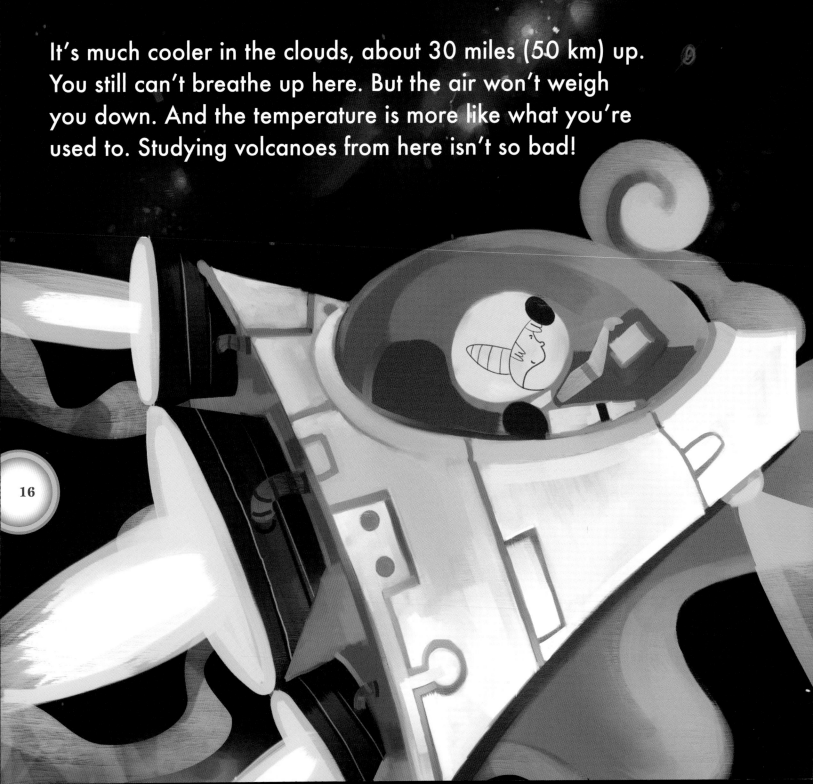

It's much cooler in the clouds, about 30 miles (50 km) up. You still can't breathe up here. But the air won't weigh you down. And the temperature is more like what you're used to. Studying volcanoes from here isn't so bad!

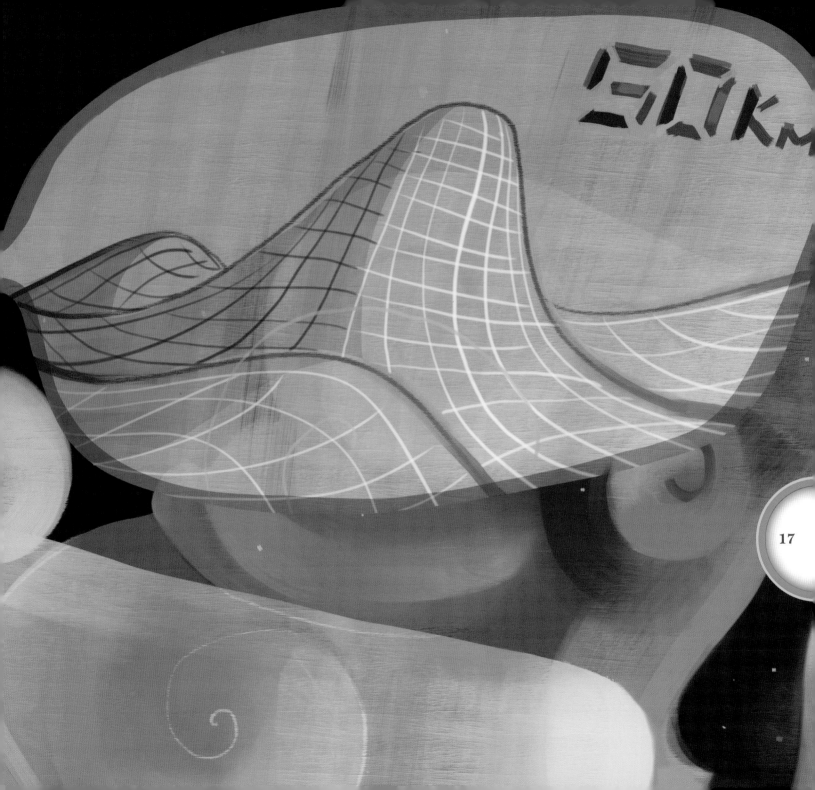

18

You can't stay here too long, if you're going to get back for the science fair.

And on Earth, you'll be able to breathe. And eat ice cream.

19

Exploring Venus's volcanoes up close is dangerous. Someday, we might explore Venus from the clouds, but you *really* wouldn't want to live there.

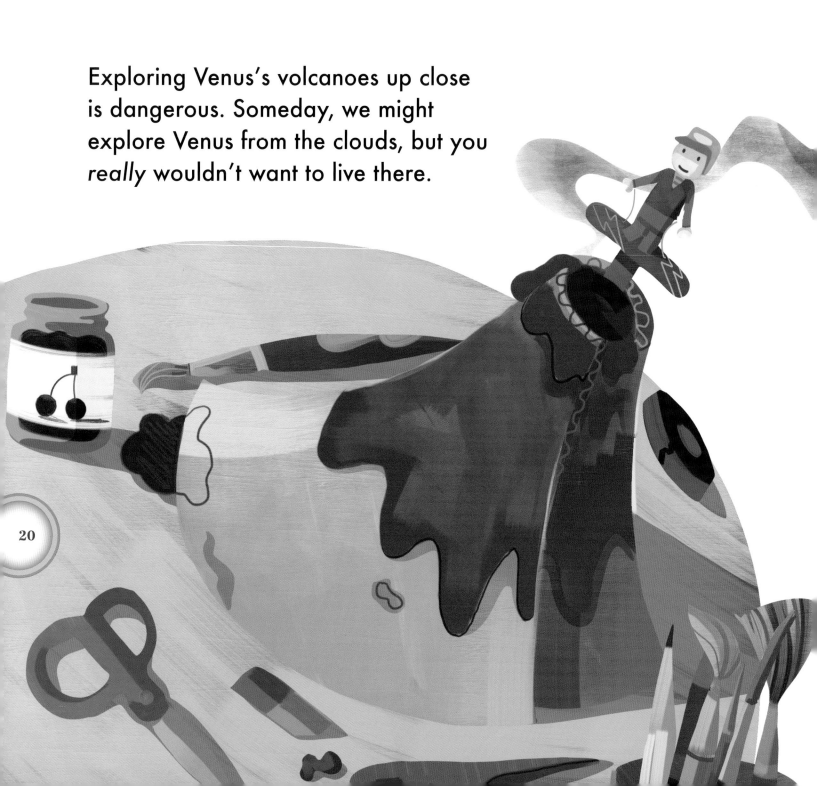

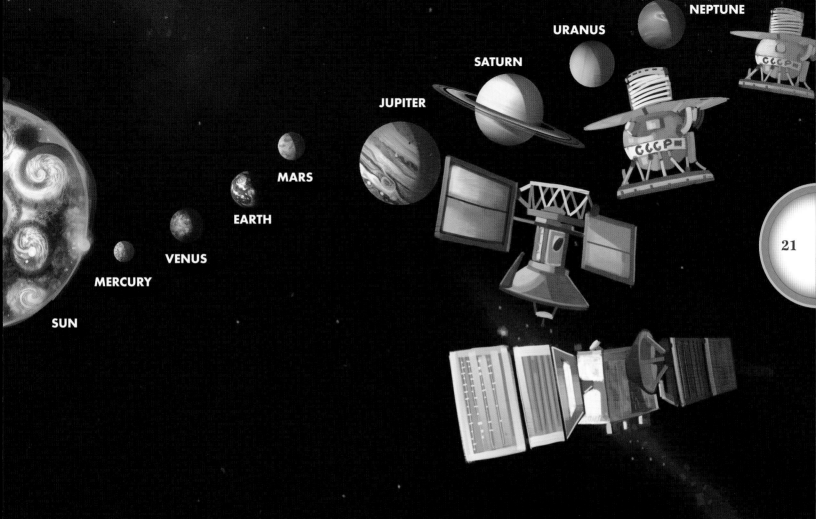

SUN

MERCURY

VENUS

EARTH

MARS

JUPITER

SATURN

URANUS

NEPTUNE

How Do We Know About Venus?

Astronauts can't actually go to Venus. A super crushproof space suit has not been invented. Instead, scientists have sent space probes. The *Venera* probes took pictures of Venus' surface. They melted after about an hour. *Magellan* orbited Venus and mapped its surface. *Venus Express* began orbiting the planet in 2006 to study the air and clouds.

Earth vs. Venus

	Earth	Venus
Position in solar system	Third from Sun	Second from Sun
Average distance from Sun	93 million miles (150 million km)	67.2 million miles (108.2 million km)
Year (time to orbit Sun)	365 days	225 days
Day (sunrise to sunrise)	24 hours	117 days
Diameter	7,926 miles (12, 756 km)	7,521 miles (12,104 km)
Mass	1	.815 x Earth (just a little smaller than Earth)
Air	Oxygen and nitrogen	Carbon dioxide and nitrogen
Water	About 70% covered with water	None
Moons	1	0
Chances of survival for an ice cream cone	Good—until someone eats it	Not a chance

Glossary

greenhouse effect The warming of the air around a planet due to gases that keep the Sun's heat from escaping.

lava The hot, liquid rock of a volcano.

space probe A robotic spacecraft that is sent into space to gather data about other planets.

sulfuric acid A heavy, colorless gas that causes corrosion of metal.

volcano A vent on the surface of a planet or moon through which lava from underground flows.

Read More

James, Lincoln. *Venus: The Masked Planet.* Our Solar System. New York: Gareth Stevens, 2011.

Owens, L.L. *Venus.* Mankato, Minn.: Child's World, 2010.

Sparrow, Giles. *Earth and the Inner Planets.* Mankato, Minn.: Smart Apple Media, 2012.

Zuchora-Walske, Christine. *Your Mission to Venus.* Edina, Minn.: Magic Wagon, 2012.

Websites

ESA Kids
http://www.esa.int/esaKIDSen/index.html
The European Space Agency offers games, coloring pages, news, and information for kids about space exploration and travel.

NASA Kids' Club
http://www.nasa.gov/audience/forkids/kidsclub/flash/
NASA Kids' Club features games, pictures, and information about astronauts and space travel.

StarChild: A Learning Center for Young Astronomers
http://starchild.gsfc.nasa.gov/docs/StarChild/
Click on Solar System to read facts about all the planets.

Venus Photos—National Geographic
http://science.nationalgeographic.com/science/photos/venus/
See beautiful photos, with captions, of the planet Venus.

About the Author

Thomas K. Adamson lives in Sioux Falls, SD, with his wife, two sons, and a dog. He has written dozens of nonfiction books for kids, many of them about planets and space. He enjoys sports, card games, reading with his sons, and pointing things out to them in the night sky.

About the Illustrator

Daniele Fabbri was born in Ravenna, Italy, in 1978. He graduated from Istituto Europeo di Design in Milan, Italy, and started his career as a cartoon animator, storyboarder, and background designer for animated series. He has worked as a freelance illustrator since 2003, collaborating with international publishers and advertising agencies.